ROBERT GRAHAM

STATUES

Travel Schedule

Walker Art Center
13 September—8 November 1981

Norton Gallery and School of Art, West Palm Beach
12 February—21 March 1982

Houston Museum of Fine Arts
15 April—6 June 1982

Joslyn Art Museum, Omaha
26 June—8 August 1982

Des Moines Art Center
7 September—17 October 1982

San Francisco Museum of Modern Art
4 November—19 December 1982

List of Lenders

Mr. and Mrs. Thomas F. Beeckler
Roy and Carol Doumani
Robert Graham
Steven Graham
Frances and Norman Lear
Byron Meyer
Robert Miller Gallery
Iris and Allen Mink
Joan and Jack Quinn
Dorothy Rosenthal Gallery
Robert A. Rowan
San Francisco Museum of Modern Art
Walker Art Center
One private collector

Copyright © Walker Art Center 1981
LC No. 81-52753
ISBN No. 0-935640-08-8

The exhibition was organized by Walker Art Center
with the aid of grants from the
National Endowment for the Arts
and the General Mills Foundation.

Dimensions are in inches; height precedes width.

ROBERT GRAHAM

Graham W. J. Beal

George W. Neubert

STATUES

Every so often an artist emerges whose work seems to run against the grain of current trends and is the result of a singular vision. Such an outsider is the California artist, Robert Graham, whose elegant, precisely rendered, yet curiously remote figurative sculpture has steadily achieved serious recognition.

In this exhibition devoted to Graham's work, Walker Art Center is privileged to present the full range of Robert Graham's editioned bronzes and a small group of the related "fragments." This exhibition, organized by the Art Center's chief curator, Graham Beal, traces a stylistic progress, from diminutive female nudes in room-like environments to the most recent bronze effigies which, though less than life-size, serenely preside over the extensive spaces they occupy.

Robert Graham has been closely involved in all aspects of the exhibition's organization. He patiently answered questions about his work during lengthy interviews and has personally made key examples of his work available for showing. Walker Art Center is particularly grateful to the individuals and museums who generously loaned Graham sculptures to this presentation. Special thanks are due Robert Graham's assistants, Noriko Fujinami and Annabella Price, who assisted with the coordination of the project.

Martin Friedman, Director
Walker Art Center

CONTENTS

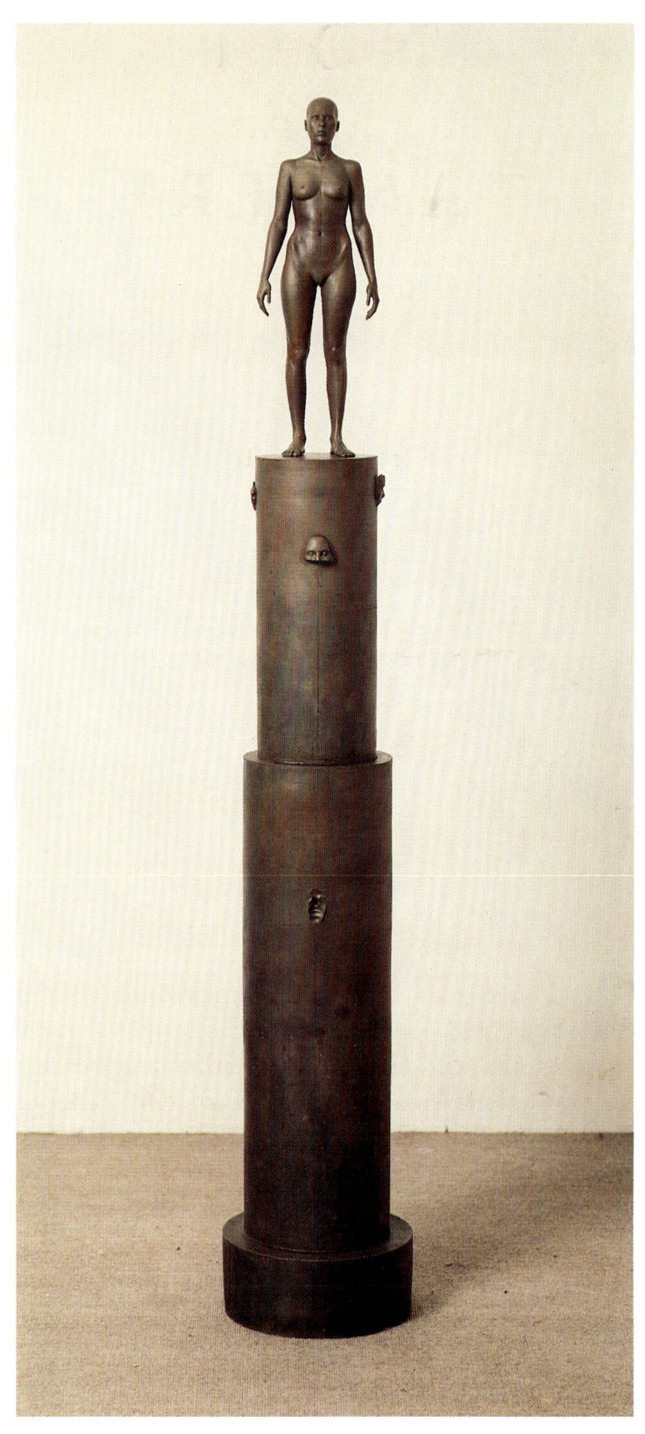

Single Figure   1973-75
bronze
67¾ x 12 diam.
Collection Roy and Carol Doumani

NOLI ME TANGERE

Graham W. J. Beal

Robert Graham is absolutely clear about the working method behind his compelling, elegantly descriptive bronzes of nudes. He says, in creating these personifications of the female figure, he is "trying to make *exactly* what I see in front of me."[1] Such a statement, as defiant as it is direct, accounts in part for the gradual increase in scale of Graham's bronze sculptures of the past decade. As his figures grew larger, he was able to invest them with greater detail which in turn heightens our fascination with their veristic qualities. The ever-increasing accuracy of his vision imbues Graham's sculptures with a distinct element of the hallucinatory. These women, life-like in detail if not in size, are simultaneously approachable and distant, symptomatic of the many opposing impulses that generate tension throughout his work: from the high-spirited beach scenes in wax of the mid-1960s, through the small bronzes of the last decade, to his most recent "environ-

1. Unless otherwise noted, all quotes are from tape recorded interviews between Robert Graham and Graham Beal, at the artist's Venice, California studio, September 1981 and February 1982.

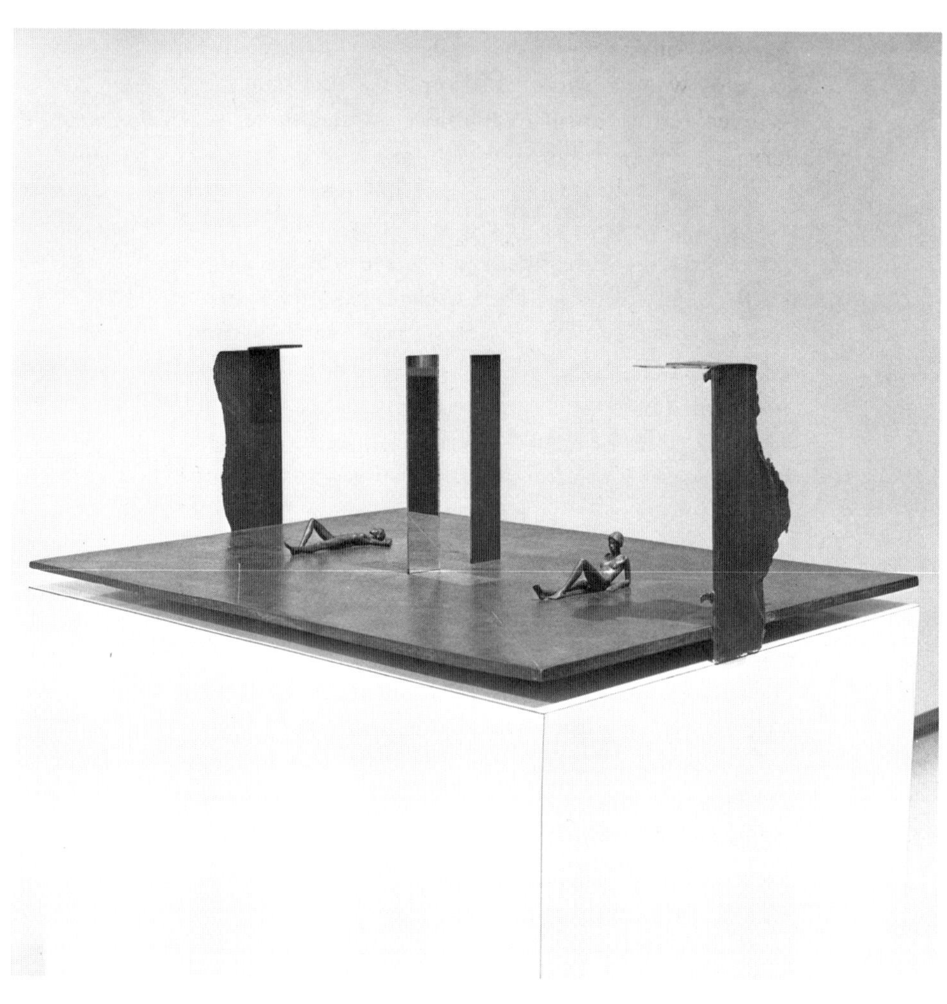

#1 Mirror   1971-73
bronze and mirror
11¾ x 35⅜ x 27½
Collection Walker Art Center

"mental" statuary. Indeed, Robert Graham's development as a sculptor can be seen in terms of his increasingly subtle exploitation of such dynamics.

Though his medium has changed from wax to bronze, the human figure remains Graham's constant theme. Even at art school in California, he says, "one week I was an abstract painter, the next week I made constructions, but I was always drawing figures." To pursue realism, especially in relation to the figure was definitely out of step in the 60s when the prevailing academy was abstraction. "There was" Graham says, "no real information available. . . 'assemblage' was very hot in those days. . . there was aluminum casting and some people were making Lynn Chadwick things with spiky shapes. . . . There wasn't any real material that I could use other than plastoline which I always used when I was a *kid*. The problem was how to make the figures set." His search for a more stable medium led to a low-fire ceramic clay that could be baked in the oven and subsequently painted. Dissatisfied with this, by 1966 he had evolved a technique for modeling in wax that he previously stained flesh color, with such details as features and hair painted in later. This method, used in a series of small tableaux of nude and nearly nude sunbathers that epitomized southern California youth and beach culture, instantly identified the artist with the Pop movement, especially with the "new" Los Angeles art scene. However, this was not a particularly accurate identification as most of these sculptures were made in San Francisco, their subjects drawn not from direct observation but from the glossy pages of *Life, Playboy* and other periodicals.

Even at this early narrative stage of Graham's career there were obvious psychological tensions throughout his work: Graham's wax miniature sybarites fascinated viewers because of the artist's meticulous attention to detail, yet no matter how closely these early figures were scrutinized, they remained as remote as they were diminutive, permanently separated from our world by their plexiglass domes. Though frequently referred to as Lilliputian, these miniscule creatures were never intended to represent a pint-sized species of humanity. In creating these hermetically-sealed environments, Graham forced the onlooker to become a voyeur whose sense of scale was challenged because the distance between him and the sculpture was indeterminate. As another Los Angeles artist, the late John Altoon neatly characterized his impression

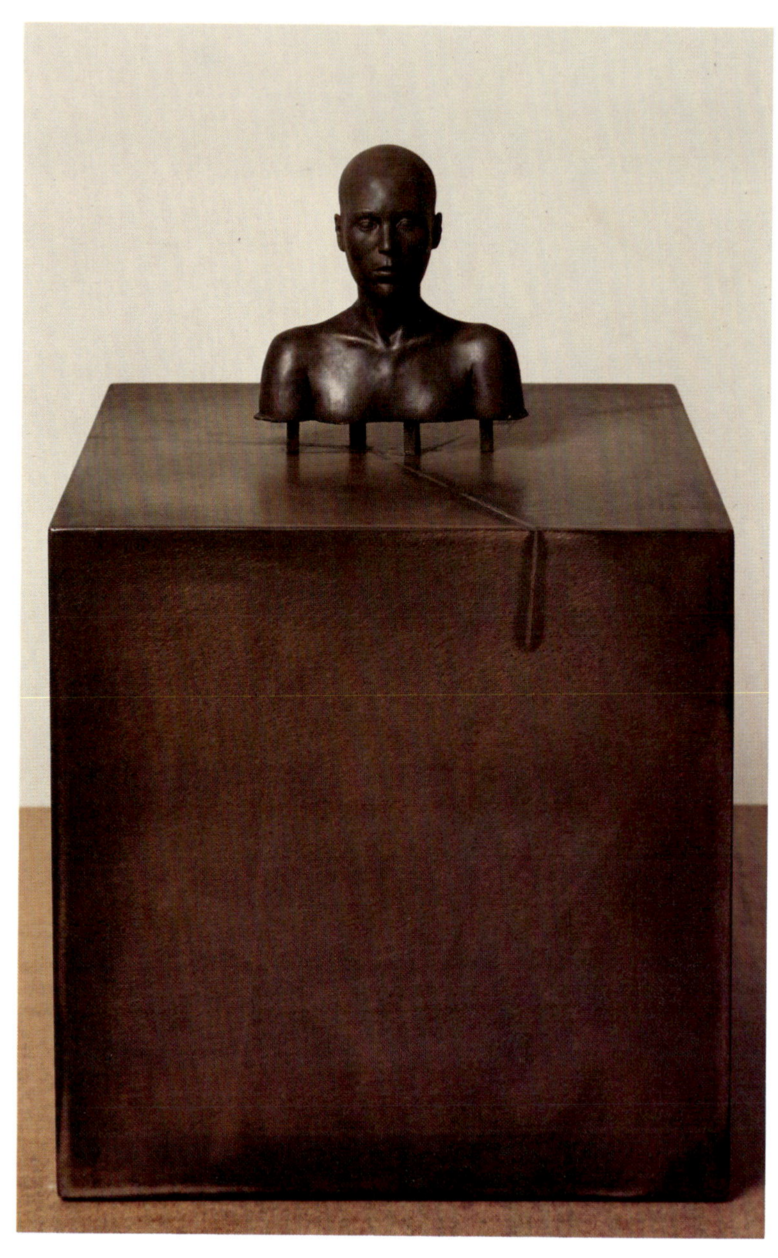

Single Head 1973
bronze
18 x 12 x 12
Private collection

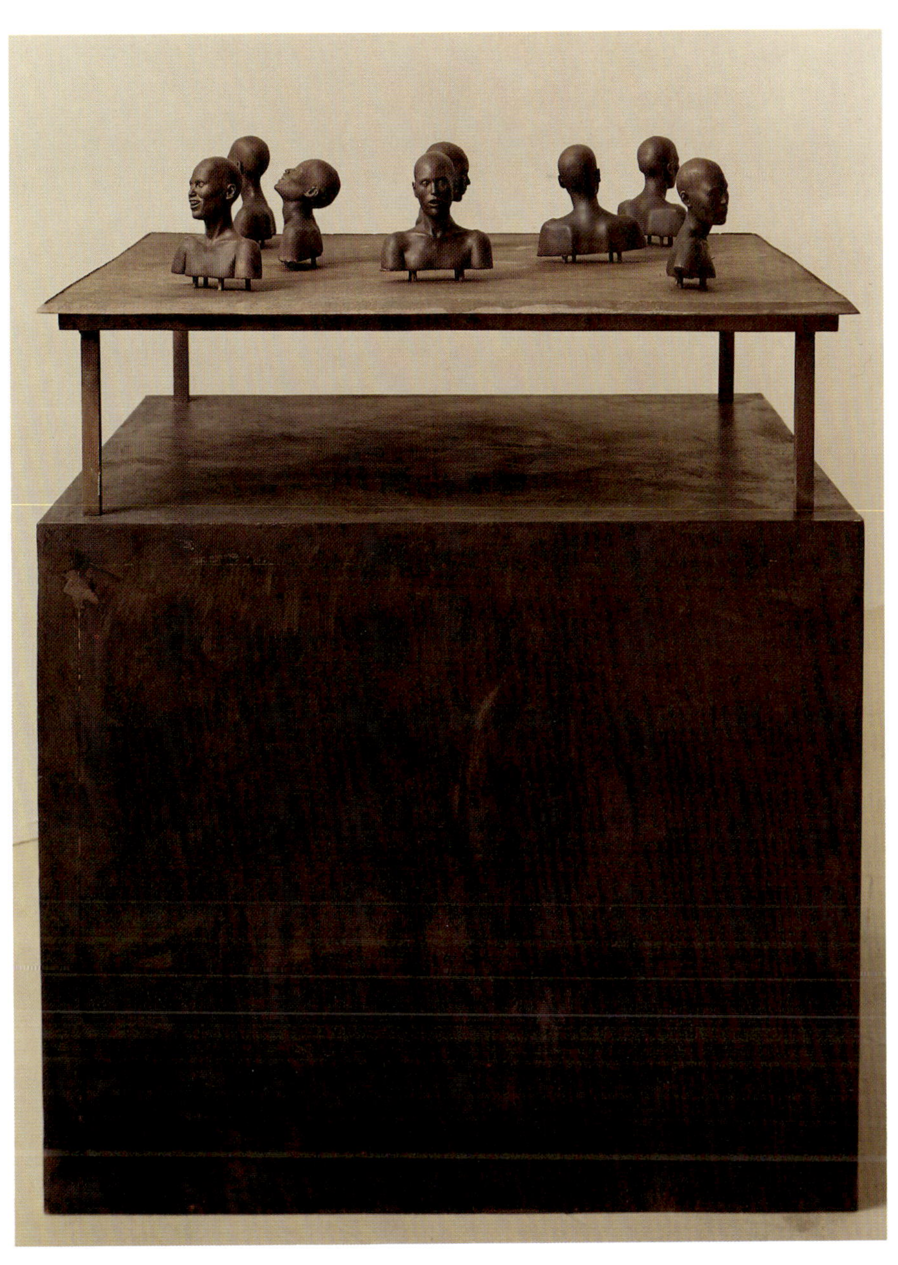

Eight Heads   1973
bronze
41½ x 33 x 33
Collection the artist

of Graham's tiny personages: "It's like seeing them real close and yet real far away." And as we look down at the activities of these "far away" figures we do not see them as insect-like specimens that, like latter-day Gullivers, we can pick up and play with; rather we are tempted to travel the necessary distance to join them.

Narrative all but disappears in a series of bronze pieces Graham made around 1970 in which the same figure can be viewed in several different positions. Reminiscent of the 19th-century photographs by Eadweard Muybridge of figures in action, these small nudes are engaged in the simplest of movements —walking, sitting down, arising. In these "stop-motion" figures Graham employed for the first time two devices that have since become central to his way of working: the camera and the casting mold. Robert Murdock, in his catalogue introduction to a 1972 Dallas Museum of Fine Arts exhibition of Graham's small wax sculptures succinctly described the artist's working method at this juncture in his career:

From a live model, Graham takes a series of reference photographs, one set being straight-on views of the standing figure from different angles; from these the master figure is modeled, and from that the mold for subsequent figures is made. A second set of reference shots shows the model going through various mechanical actions; these are used as the source for the specific poses. By immersing the cast wax figures in warm water, they become malleable and can be bent and formed into a given pose; once this has been achieved, Graham does a good deal of detail work, making subtle refinements in the figure. By photographing different models, each of whom executes basic actions in a different way, Graham has assembled a vast collection of possible sources.

In these early works the figure itself is the subject. The artist's paramount interest in nuance of gesture is unmistakable and, by using two-sided mirrors in the final wax pieces, he further drew attention to these basic concerns.

Wax figures are easily damaged and, motivated by practical as well as aesthetic considerations, Graham decided in 1971 to try bronze. "I just got tired" he says, "of things breaking and, anyway, by that time, I was working with a very spare situation—just a mirror and two figures. I thought bronze would work because there was no more descriptive coloring in the figures." The first bronze, *Mirror No. 1*, made between 1971 and 1973 is clearly an extension of ideas hinted at in earlier wax pieces. Though no plexiglass covers *Mirror No. 1*, Graham's two irregularly-contoured vertical brackets create the sense of a room in which two small figures lie parallel to one another. Their poses are identical below the waist, but one sits up, resting

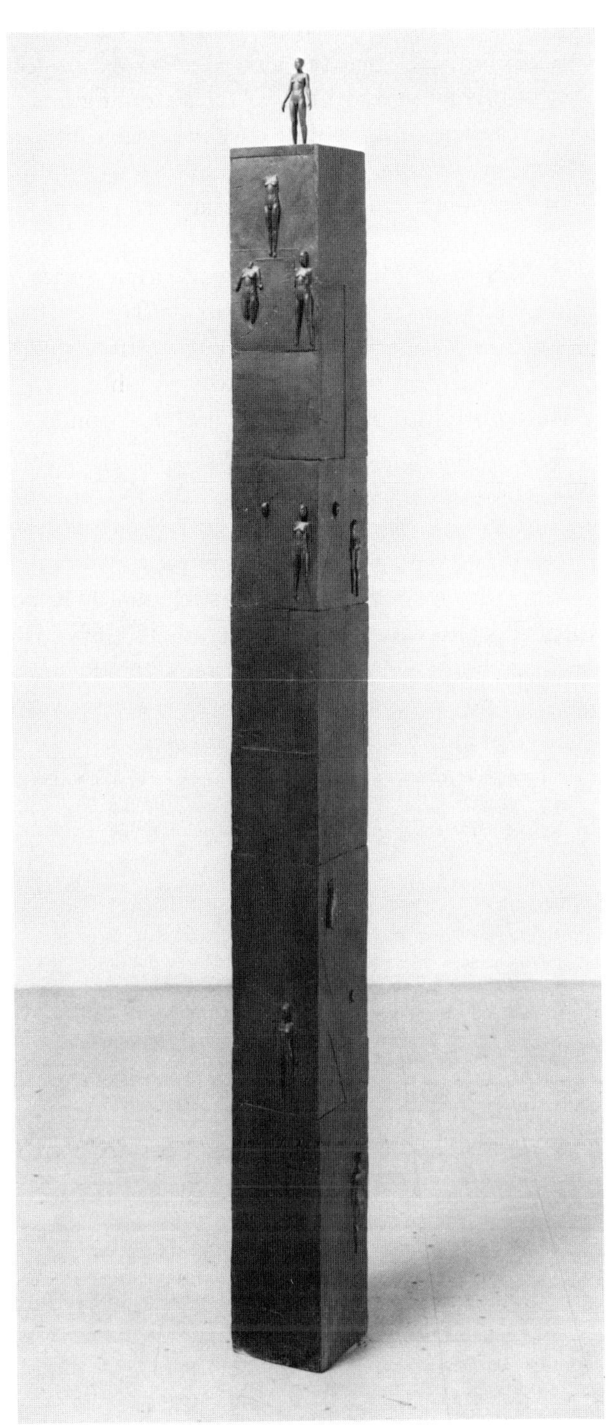

Column #1   1974
bronze
81¼ x 6¼ x 6¼
Collection the artist

on her elbows, the other lies flat, hands clasped behind her head. Between them are two tall mirrors, one facing each nude. By moving around the work the spectator can make the reflection of the nearer figure intersect with that of the further one, thus causing either figure to "sit up" or "lie down." The artist has remarked that, despite the title, "the pieces are not about mirrors; if they were, it would be a trick." Rather the mirrors serve to draw attention to each figure. In giving two alternative positions for the lower half of the body, Graham suggests an infinite number of poses and introduces motion into his composition.

A significant shift in approach is seen in the 1973 *Single Head*. Here Graham presents only the head and shoulders of the figure: what, in academic art, would be called a "bust", but there the similarities end because this sculpture is presented on four short stilts mounted on a 12-inch cube. There is another departure from academic procedures; the sensitive, life-like portrayal of face and shoulders is counteracted by the notable absence of two important life-imbuing features: the head is hairless and the eyes have no pupils. Nevertheless, the carefully-modeled skull is brought to the same degree of finish as the rest of the figure.

In *Eight Heads*, a 1973 work, Graham used the same approach, but each head is tilted at a different angle and bears a distinct facial expression—laughing, smiling, grimacing, and so on. Strange mixtures of traditional statuary and science-fiction humanoids, these are eerie personages. Cleanly cut off below the shoulders and mounted like trophies, these bald, sightless creatures do not seem to be fragments of complete figures, but seem complete in themselves, beings from another world. Graham has replaced the viewer's physical separation from his sculpture with psychological distance. Though Graham understands how a viewer could come to such an interpretation, this was not in his mind when he made this totemistic object. Certain features were omitted because, he says, "I didn't know how to make the hair, how to deal with it. . . . I can appreciate that it scares people but it doesn't scare me. I can see that, as a representation of a bald figure, it *is* weird but I *never* see it as a bald figure—I just didn't put any hair on it." Despite the disconcerting effect of Graham's sculpture, for the first time his works begin to assume classical overtones. The exquisite features of these heads, or lack of them, forces us to see their subjects as types rather than as in-

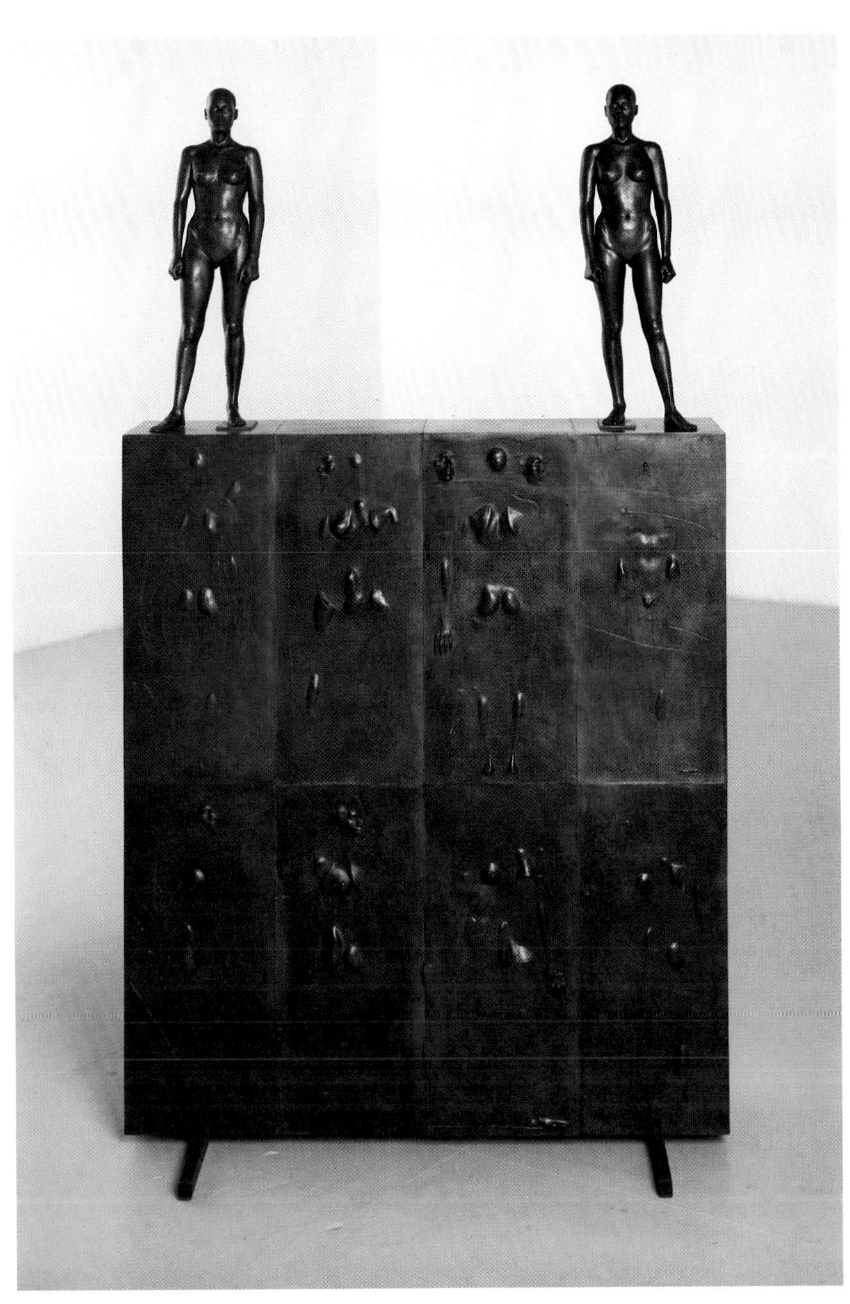

Mirror Figure   1973-76
bronze
60 x 35 x 8½
Collection Joan and Jack Quinn

dividuals. Again, much of the dynamism in such sculpture derives from our ambiguous relation to them.

Graham greatly extended his formal repertoire in a series of elaborate bronzes begun in 1973 that feature standing figures reminiscent of votary statues mounted on sizable "bases" each adorned with relief elements deriving from the figure. In making these figures Graham realized he was also "making tools;" and that, by using them as stamps, he could make impressions in slabs of clay. Such impressions became the basis for molds for producing relief elements which, when cast, were then incorporated into the base. In the 1974 *Column No. 1*, a small figure stands, legs slightly apart, arms held out from the thighs, atop a tall narrow rectangular column. Some relief forms reproduced the full figure above; others are variants. Overall the work alludes to the process of creation and, as with *Mirror No. 1*, the two or three options actually seen in the finished sculptures represent an infinite variety.

A major change in scale occurs in two works of this "series," *Mirror Figure* (1973-76) and *Single Figure* (1973-75). Larger and more forbidding than their predecessors, it is apparent, for the first time in Graham's bronzes that we are looking at a specific individual: a bony, slightly ungainly young woman. Graham's subjects are not professional models and when he sees someone whose form intrigues him, he may ask her to pose. There follow long sessions in which Graham makes studies of the model in clay. He also takes copious photographs and, in recent years, has videotaped the model standing, sitting and in motion. He works with his models until they are completely self-absorbed, oblivious of his presence; it is understandable, then, why his bronze figures seem to exist in a world of their own. They are distant, in a state near transfiguration. Altoon's characterization of the diminutive beach people—close up yet far away—holds true for the more recent bronzes.

The sense of real flesh and bone is greatly heightened in two 1976-77 works, *Torso I* and *Torso II*. Again, larger in scale than previous work, the details of these bodies are lovingly modeled, each dimple and contour recorded. But, Graham never achieves such acute description merely to drift into idealization. Such intensified reality is counteracted by the abrupt, even brutal truncation of the figure and, once more, the viewer is presented with a dichotomy: Graham's torsos are not fragments—relics of once-complete figures. No romantic spirit emanates from them; they are crystalline forms rendered in sharp focus, presented in a format verging on the abstract. And there are further, disconcerting overtones. Confronted with such unerring realism the temptation is to ask why the other parts are missing. Though not a significant factor in the artist's mind, possible interpretations lead to consideration of the figure as totem, as partly-realized goddess or perhaps some sort of victim. As in *Single Head*, Graham has taken a traditional classical format and by a combination of astonishing realism and drastic editing has created entities that simultaneously attract and rebuff the viewer.

With the three *Lise* sculptures of 1977, based on an adolescent California model who posed for Graham for several years, he returned to the complete figure to adopt the convention he still favors: a figure approximately three feet tall on a minimal geometric base. In the *Lise* series the degree of naturalism is intensified and, apart from the hair, the figure is fully modeled. Poses range from the passivity of *Lise I*, to the near swagger of *Lise II*, to the defiance of *Lise III*, but each combines languor and intensity. For the first time, we sense the figures observing us as we observe them. If the scale and context of the mid-70s nudes recall votary statuary, those from 1977 onward belong to a more general "tradition" that the artist has identified for himself. Referring to sculpture from such disparate vanished civilizations as Egypt and Cambodia, Graham says, "People have always used this size. . . and you only make them bigger or smaller for specific reasons. . . . You have smaller votary figures to keep in your pocket and bigger things—civic—to scare you." In discussing his own work, such references to ancient art tend to outnumber those to contemporary work. Consequently, unlike that of such contemporaries as John de Andrea and Duane Hansen, Graham's sculpture cannot be closely related to Pop or photorealist trends. De Andrea's life-size studio nudes and Hansen's relentlessly clinical portrayals of everyday people are awesome examples of one-to-one realism. They impress, at first glance, because they seem to be real people. But shock is an important part of their aesthetic and closer inspection only serves to reveal *how* they are made and that they are, in fact, *not* real; in the last analysis, we delight in their verisimilitude but do not relate to them as more than reproductions

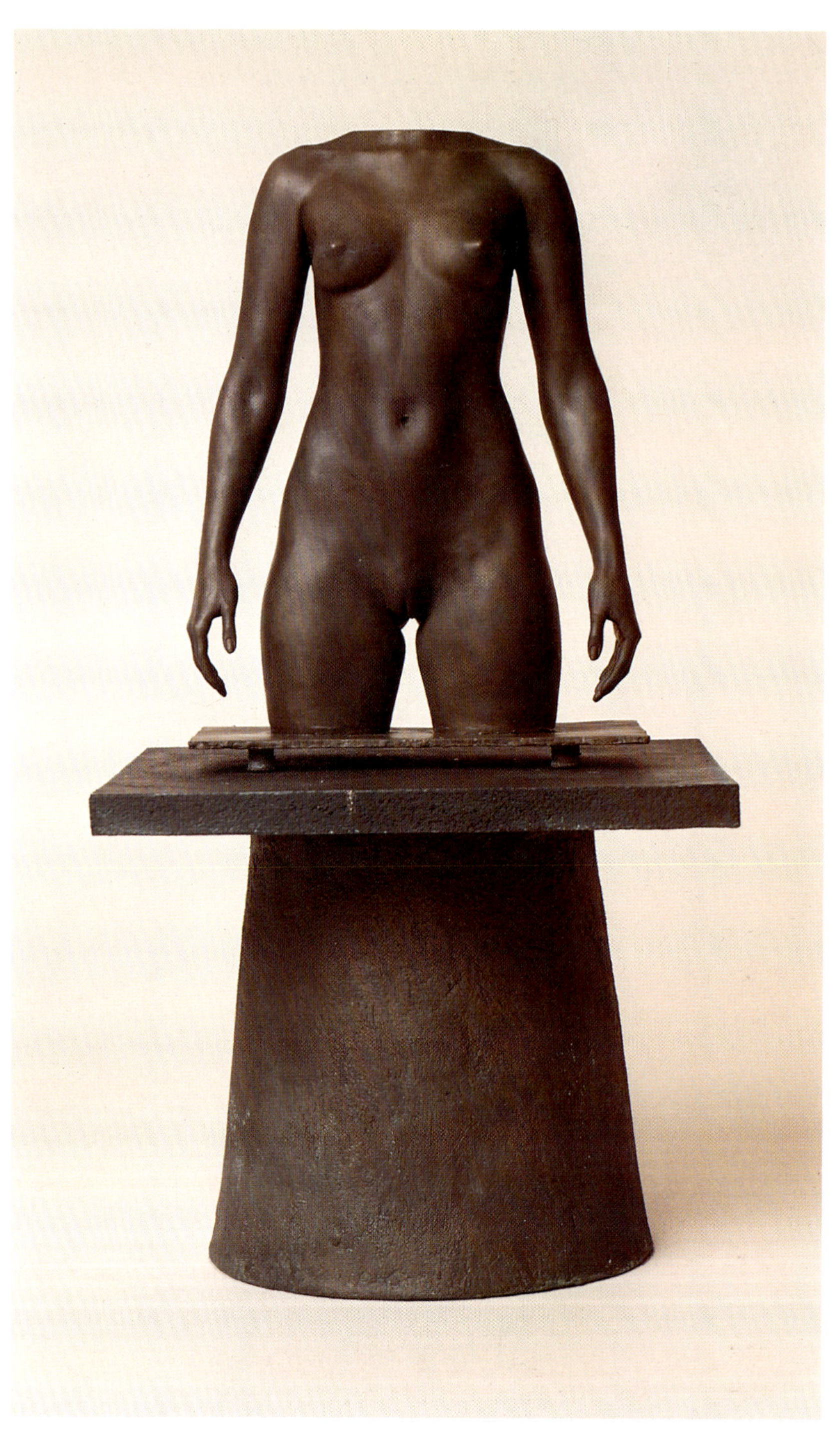

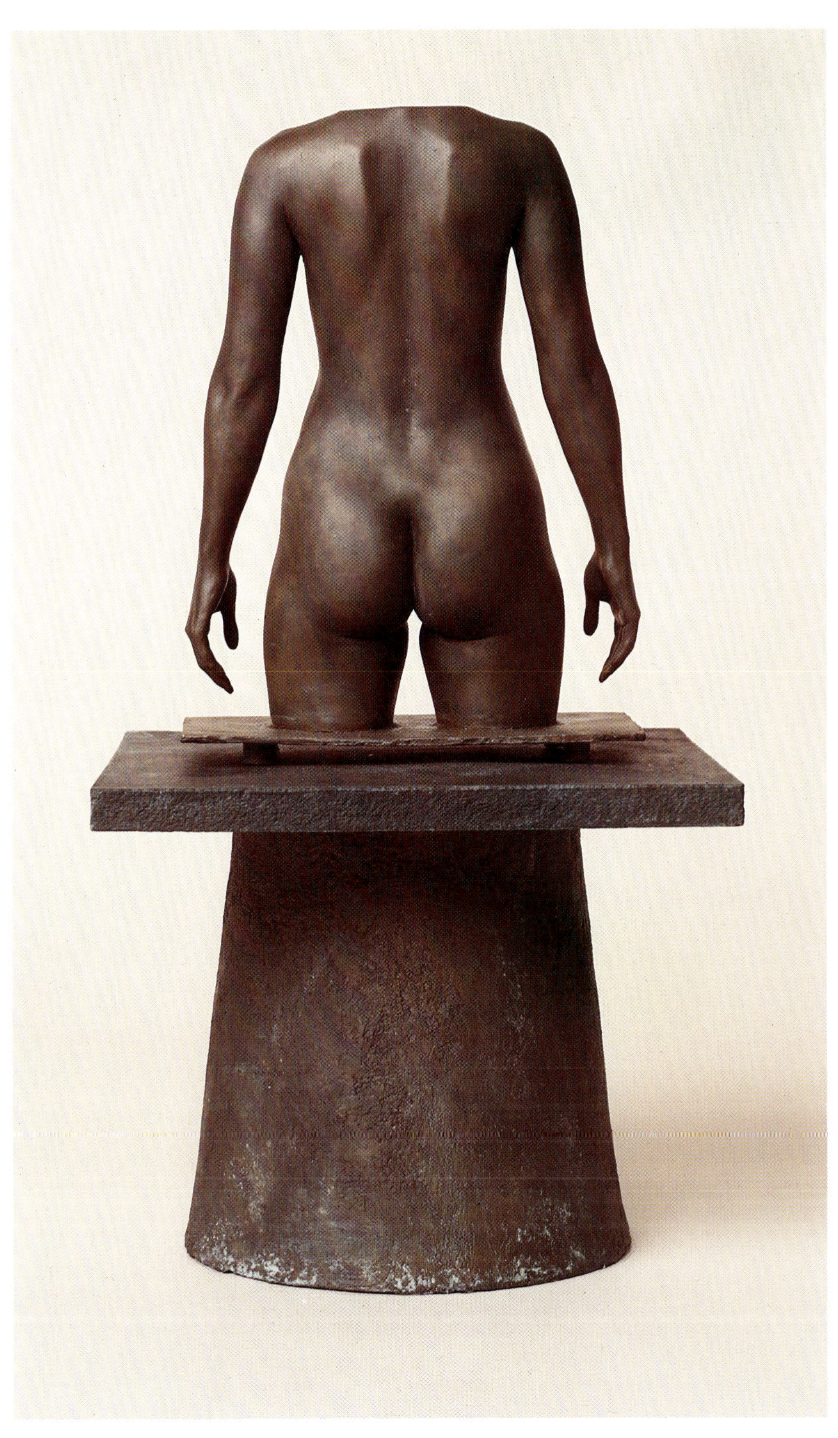

Torso I   1975-76
bronze
22 x 9 x 4
Collection Robert A. Rowan

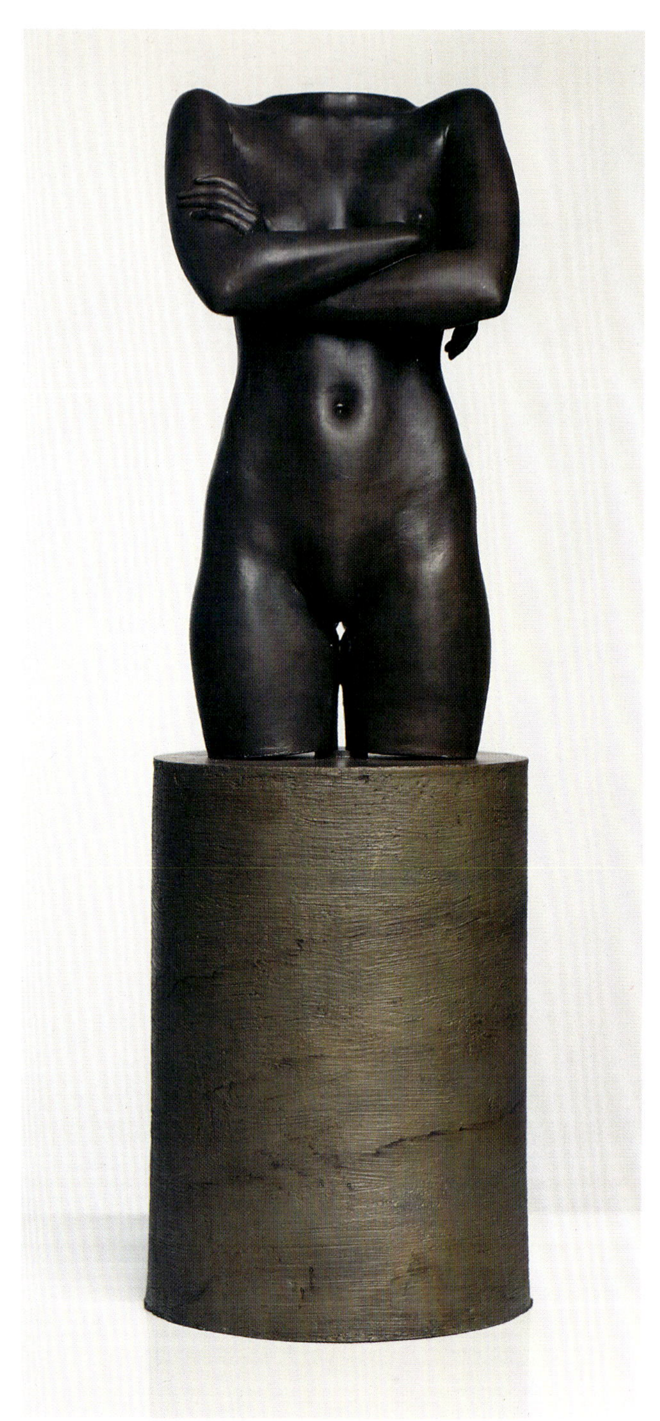

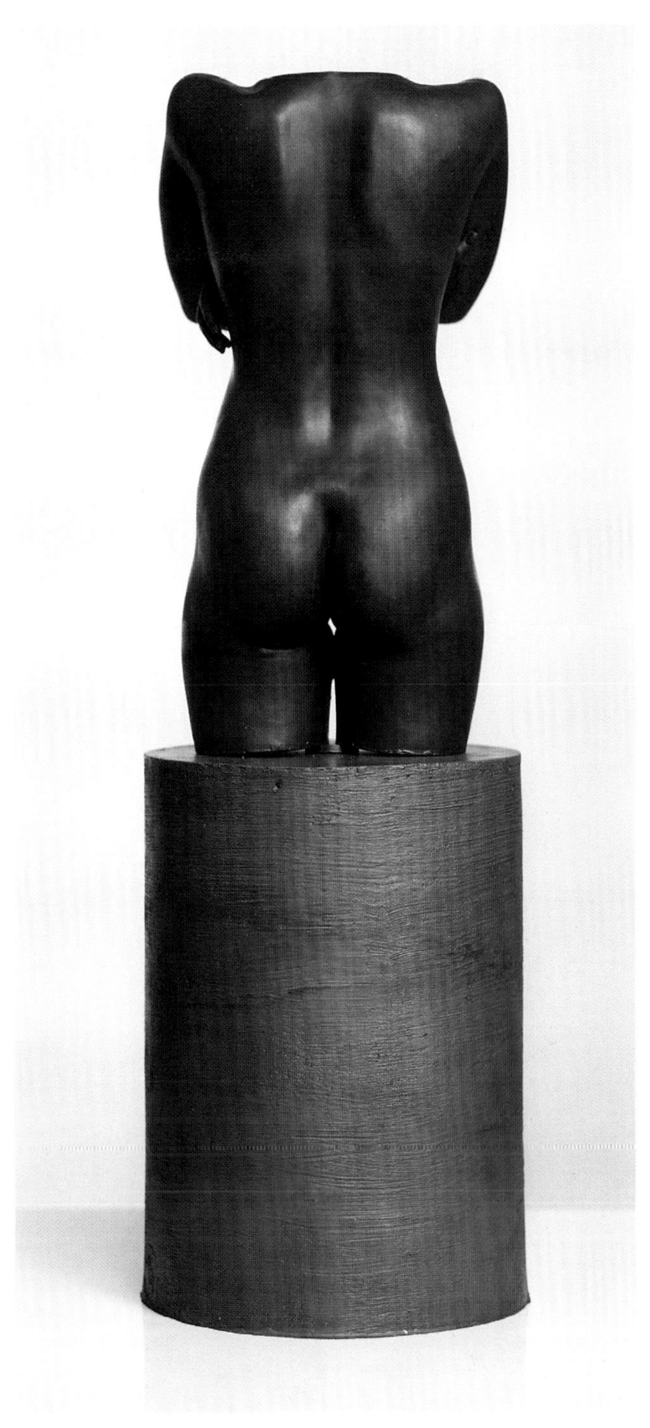

Torso II   1976-77
bronze
20¼ x 6 x 4⅜
Courtesy Dorothy Rosenthal Gallery

of other people. In Graham's work the opposite holds true: the less than life-size bronze figures become, somehow, *more* real as we examine them. Our awareness of his craft gives way, slowly but surely, to a sense of life within the figure. Though he claims he is simply trying to reproduce what was before him in the studio—a nude female—by reducing its scale he has also distilled the figure to its essence. Any by simplifying he intensified it so that it becomes "a metaphor for the human spirit."

Lise Dance Figure I and *Lise Dance Figure II* (1977) are Graham's most recent efforts to depict physical movement. These dancing figures, above eye level on their attenuated pedestals, are totally at ease. *Lise Dance Figure I* holds one leg horizontally, as if carrying out some practice routine. *Lise Dance Figure II* raises one leg and glances over her shoulder to examine the side of her foot, self-absorbed and oblivious to our presence. Once again, Graham puts the viewer in the position of voyeur.

A wide spectrum of bronze patinas is available to the sculptor but, to color his statues, Graham uses oil paint. No longer concerned with naturalism but with tonal values he prefers a fairly narrow range of purples, grays and greens. The early small wax figures had local details such as lipstick and suntan marks as did those in the glossy magazines he borrowed them from. When he shifted to using his own black and white photos for research he was no longer concerned with approximating flesh color. And as Graham says, "In sculpture color doesn't matter at all because once it turns a corner it becomes another color and you never see it the same way again, anyway." Even so, the bloodless hues he now favors have the effect of counteracting the realistic modeling of the nudes, further contributing to the emotional distance between viewer and figure.

Subsequent sculpture such as *Heather* (1979), *Stephanie* (1980), *Cherie* (1980) are essentially motionless goddesses. These women stand legs apart, arms out slightly from the body. The largest sculptures he has made, they too, demonstrate the artist's developing ability to record what is before him. "That's not" Graham says, "where it is going to stop. I'm going to make variations. What I have with these figures are tools that I can use. . . like a repertory company. But I'm not just waiting for something to happen. I think they have everything in them."

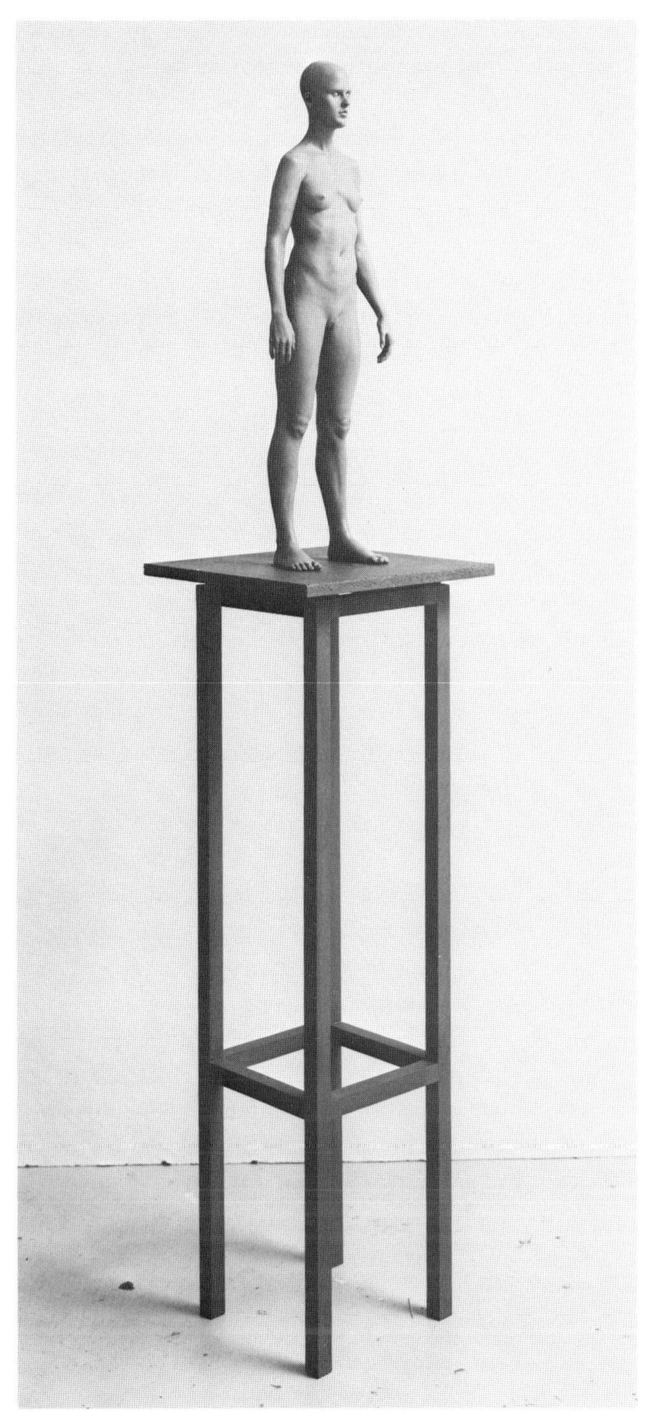

Lise I   1977
bronze
67 x 9¼ x 6
Collection Frances and Norman Lear

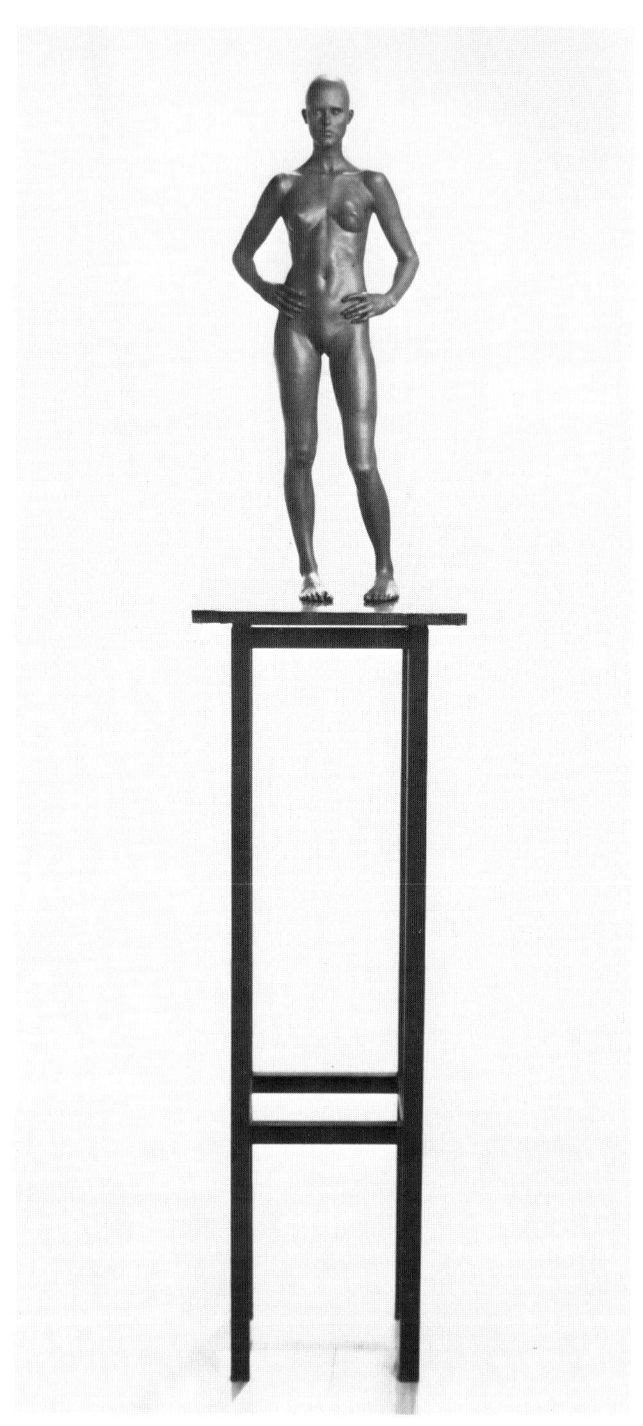

Lise II   1977
bronze
68 x 10 x 5½
Collection Iris and Allen Mink

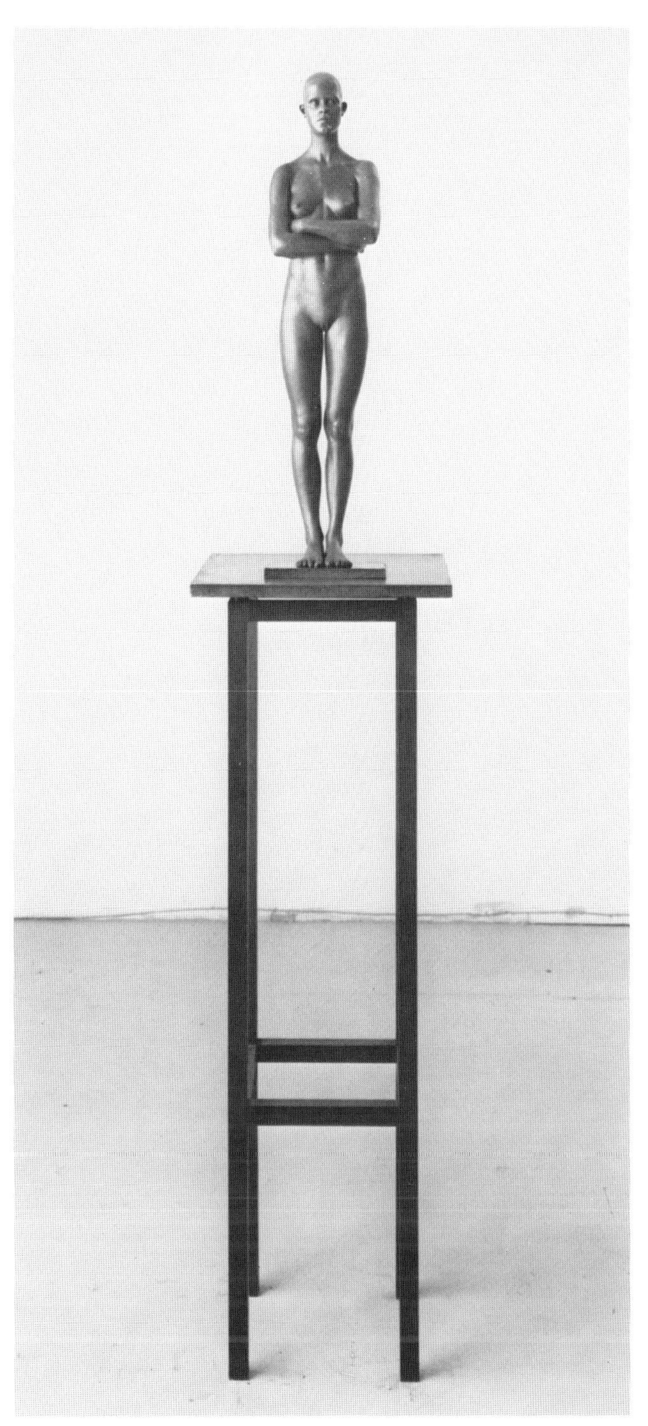

Lise III   1977
bronze
68 x 6 x 5
Collection Mr. and Mrs. Thomas F. Beeckler

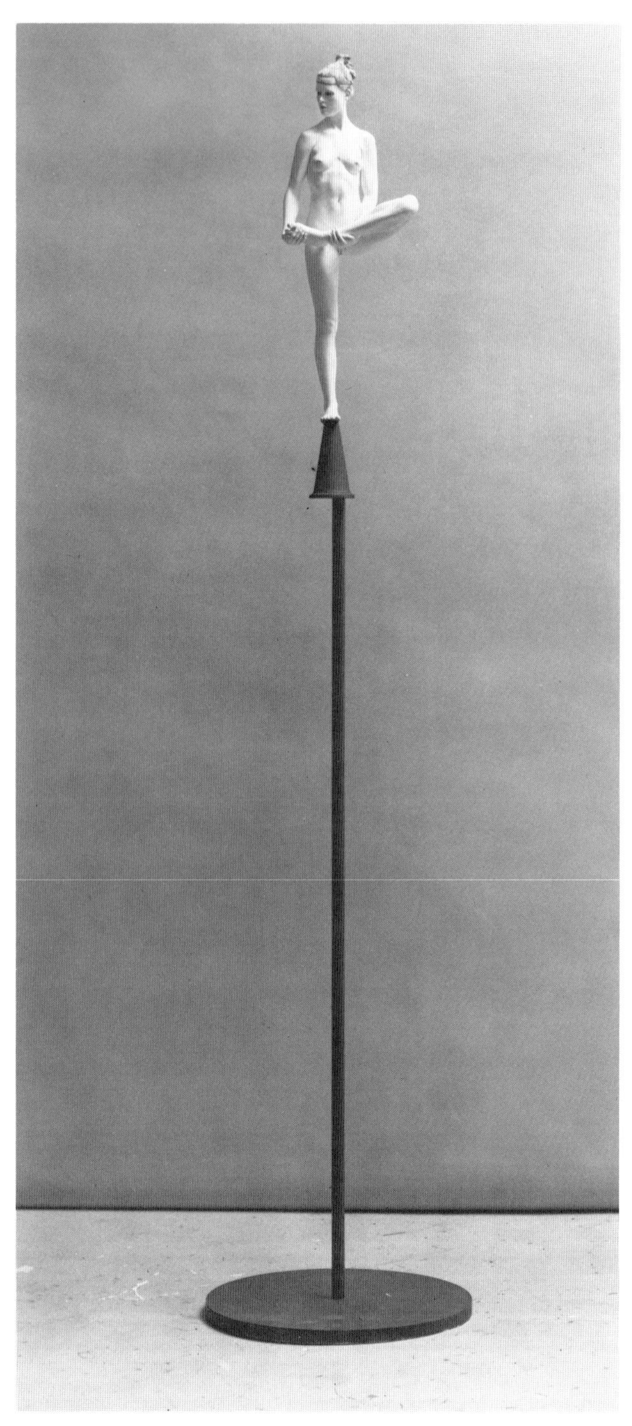

Lise Dance Figure I   1979
painted bronze with silk
93 x 11 x 7
Collection Byron Meyer

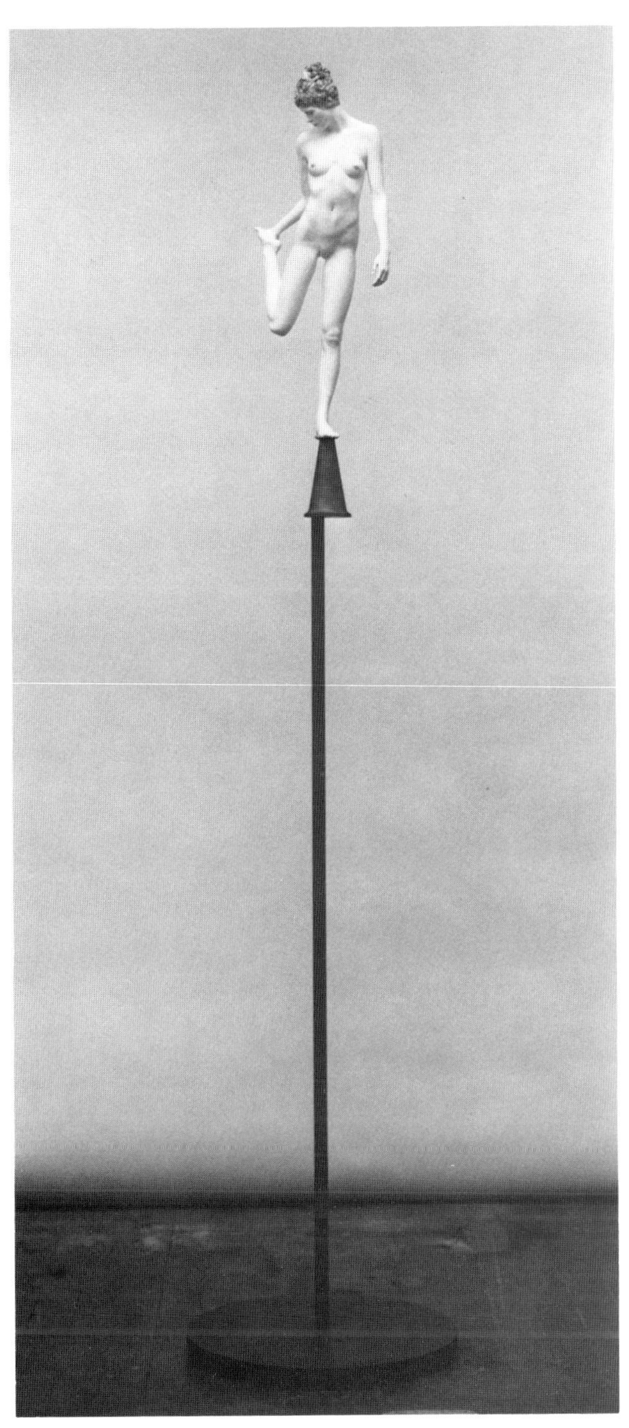

Lise Dance Figure II   1979
painted bronze with silk
93 x 14 x 6
Collection San Francisco Museum of Modern Art

The strength of Graham's bronze nudes derives from his ability to transpose as accurately as possible the model in his studio into permanent form. Through intense observation and without recourse to obvious stylization he distills the figures to a hallucinatory presence simultaneously real and idealized. *Lise,* and all the others, are rich with association, recalling, on the one hand, female deities of ancient civilization, on the other, a more sentimental rendition of the human figure: Victorian table-top statuary. But Graham works in such a direct, one-to-one fashion with his model that the possibility of much precise stylistic influence being brought to bear on him is limited. In terms of contemporary art, Graham's work has always been something of an anomaly and, even in these post-modernist days when artists and architects are once more finding meaning in classical motifs, it remains distinct. Though admitting that his work would not look the way it does without "Brancusi, Moore, Marini and all the others," his sculpture, he continues, "has nothing to do with style. It does have something to do with the way something is seen by a particular culture but I am being as straight as possible with these figures, making them as I see them. . . and I get better at it, better at being able to see."

Such an approach certainly results in a kind of "stylelessness" but there is a great deal going on beneath the realist "skin." Graham's art is based on a series of subtle, overlapping oppositions. Far more so than his early beach-scene fantasies in wax, the bronze figures of the 70s are inviting yet inhibiting. Increase in size and scale has made them no more accessible, for, by a strange paradox, Graham's tightly-focused realism results in a form of idealization. Though distinct, recognizable individuals, the women depicted are inevitably transformed—through the bronze medium and reduced scale—into generic beings: types of beauty. In turn, this idealized beauty verges on the unearthly. Confronted by a Graham figure, the viewer is caught between the desire to embrace and the impulse to worship and, more than anything else, becomes aware of the subtle, underlying ambiguities that give Robert Graham's statues their own particular sense of life.

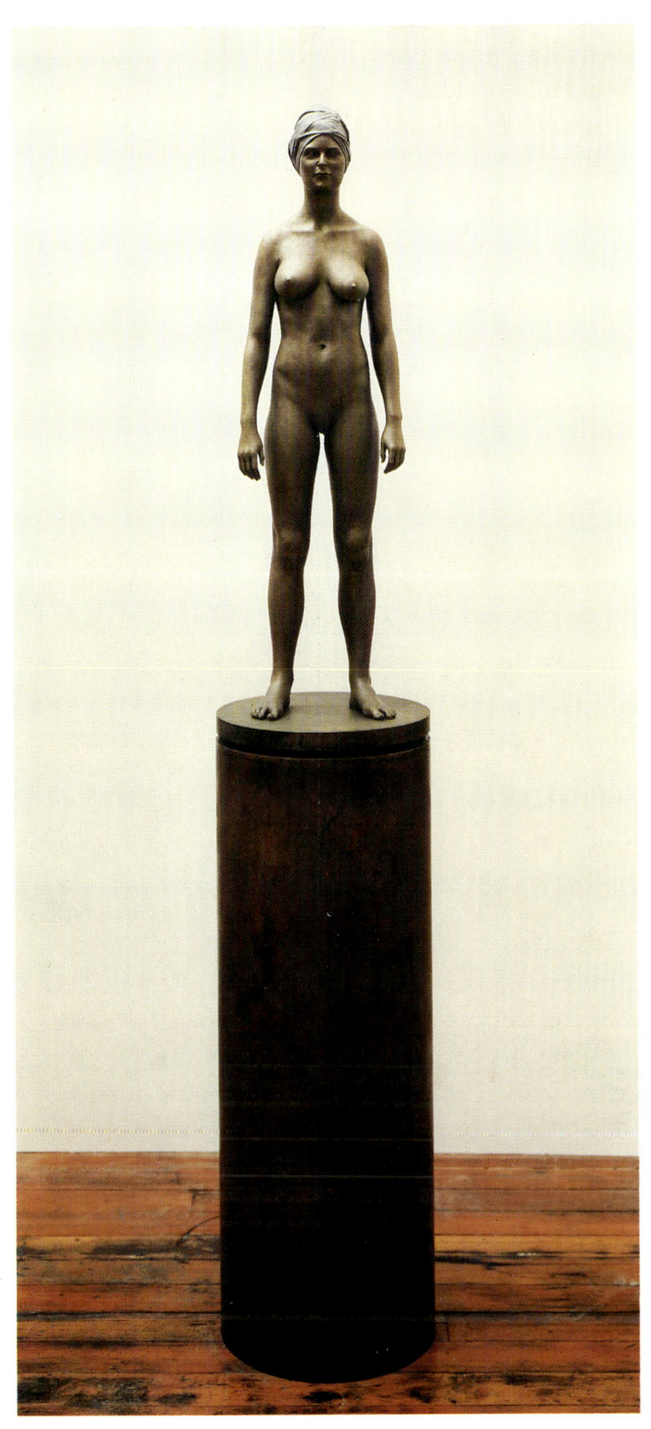

Heather   1979
bronze
68 x 9 x 4
Collection Frances and Norman Lear

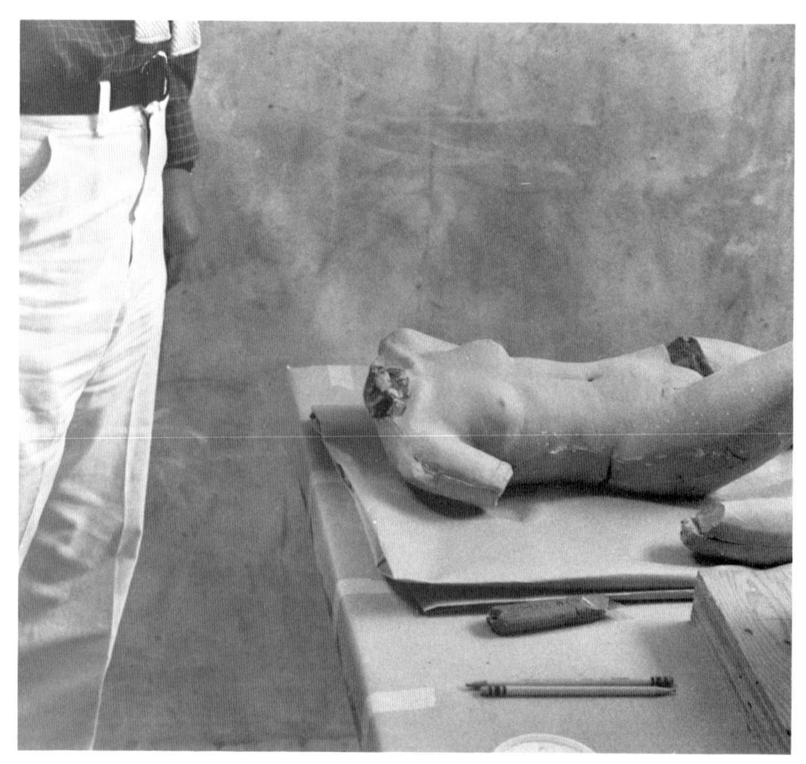

THE FRAGMENTS

Handmade Found Objects

The complicated process of casting bronze sometimes goes wrong. Airpockets, for example, can form and impede the flow of liquid metal; as a result the figures emerge in an incomplete state.

The artist wastes nothing, however, and these partial forms become raw material for the fragments: a related yet distinct aspect of Graham's work in bronze. Graham has described these as his "found objects" and, although he created the original forms, he regards them as "manifestations of something I somehow never made. . . they are surprises to me." As such, the fragments, relying upon accident and discovery, represent the "flip side" of Graham's working method exemplified by the tightly-controlled editioned bronzes.

Invariably painted pale hues of green, grey and purple and occasionally adorned with gold leaf or wire, the fragments are poignant images that combine a sense of fragility with jewel-like perfection.

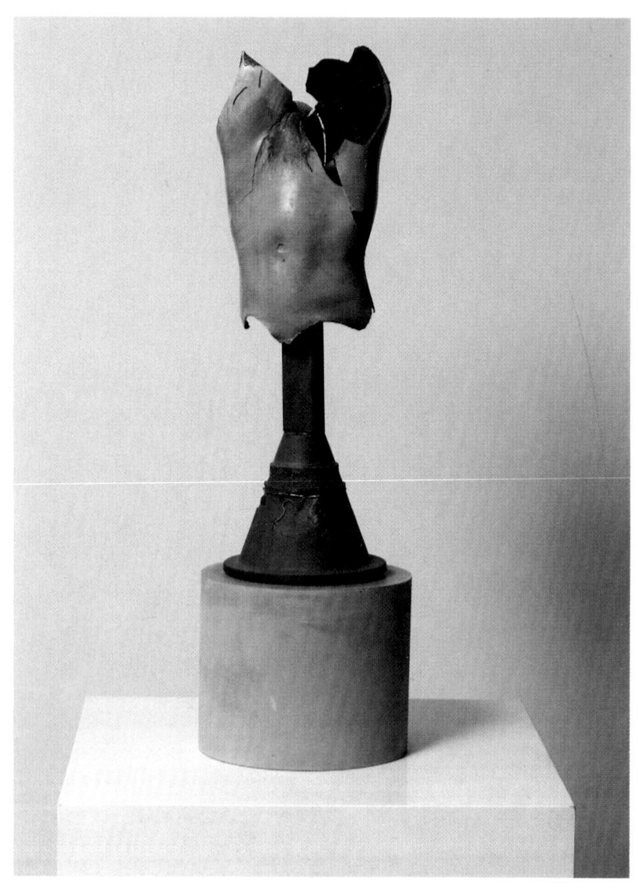

Fragment Painted 5-14-80   1980
bronze, oil paint, copper wire with cement base
24¾ x 6¼ x 6
Collection the artist

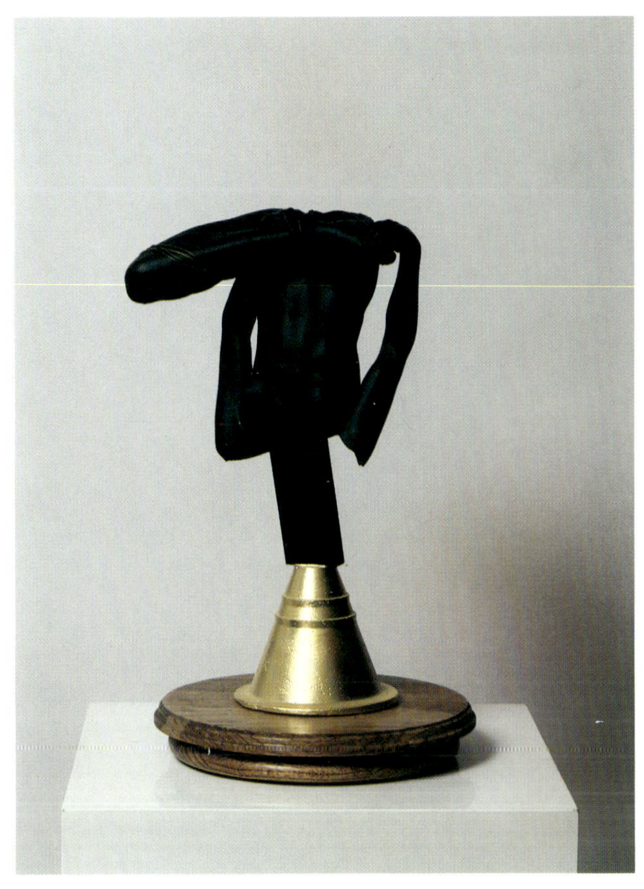

Fragment Painted 5-2-80   1980
bronze, oil paint, gold leaf, copper wire
17¾ x 10¼ x 7¾
Collection Roy and Carol Doumani

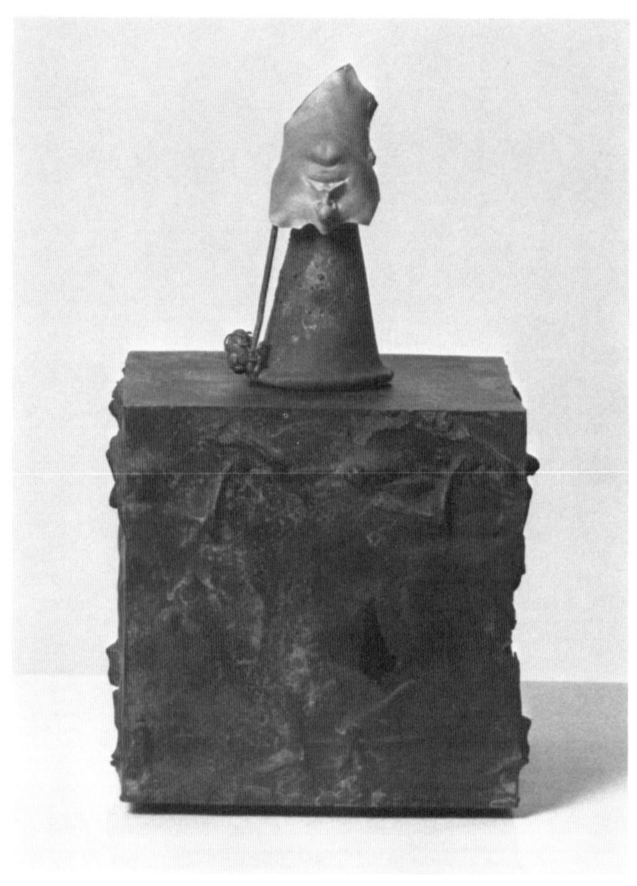

Fragment Painted 5-27-80   1980
bronze, oil paint, copper wire with bronze base
13⅛ x 7 x 7
Collection the artist

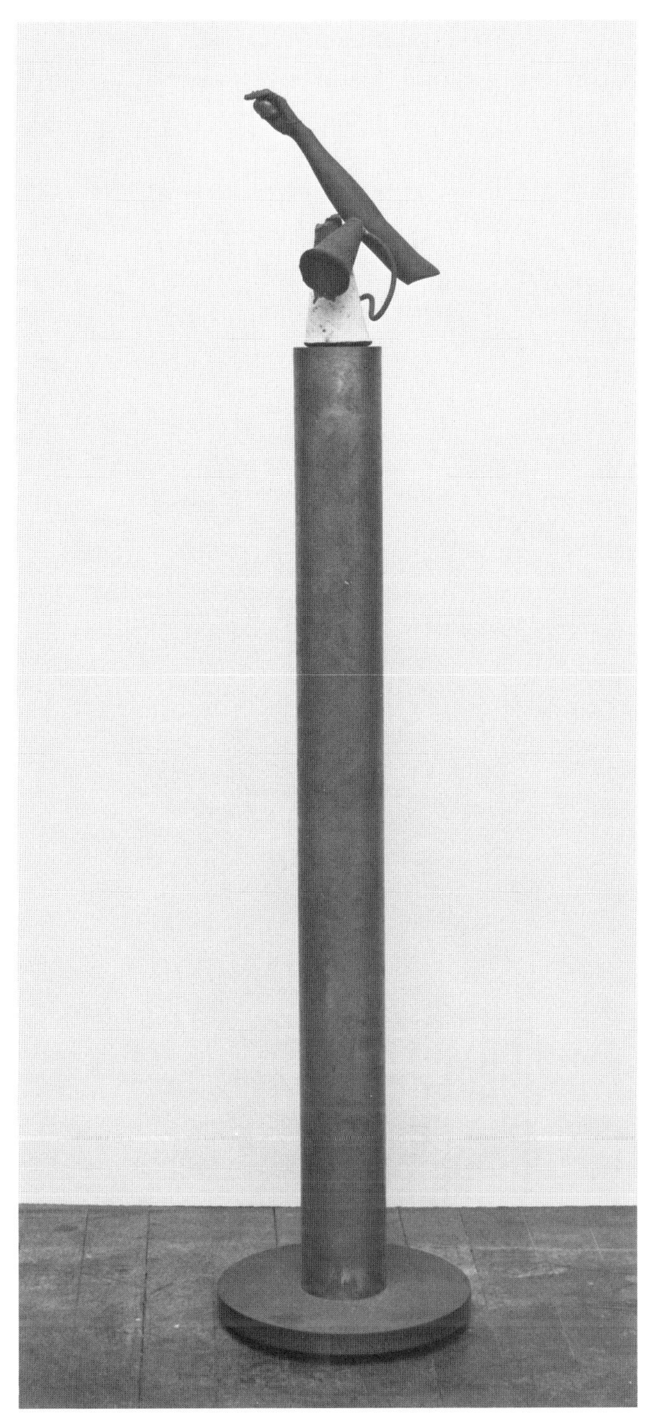

Fragment 5-19-80   1980   (not in exhibition)
bronze, copper wire with copper base
55½ x 9 x 5½
Collection the artist

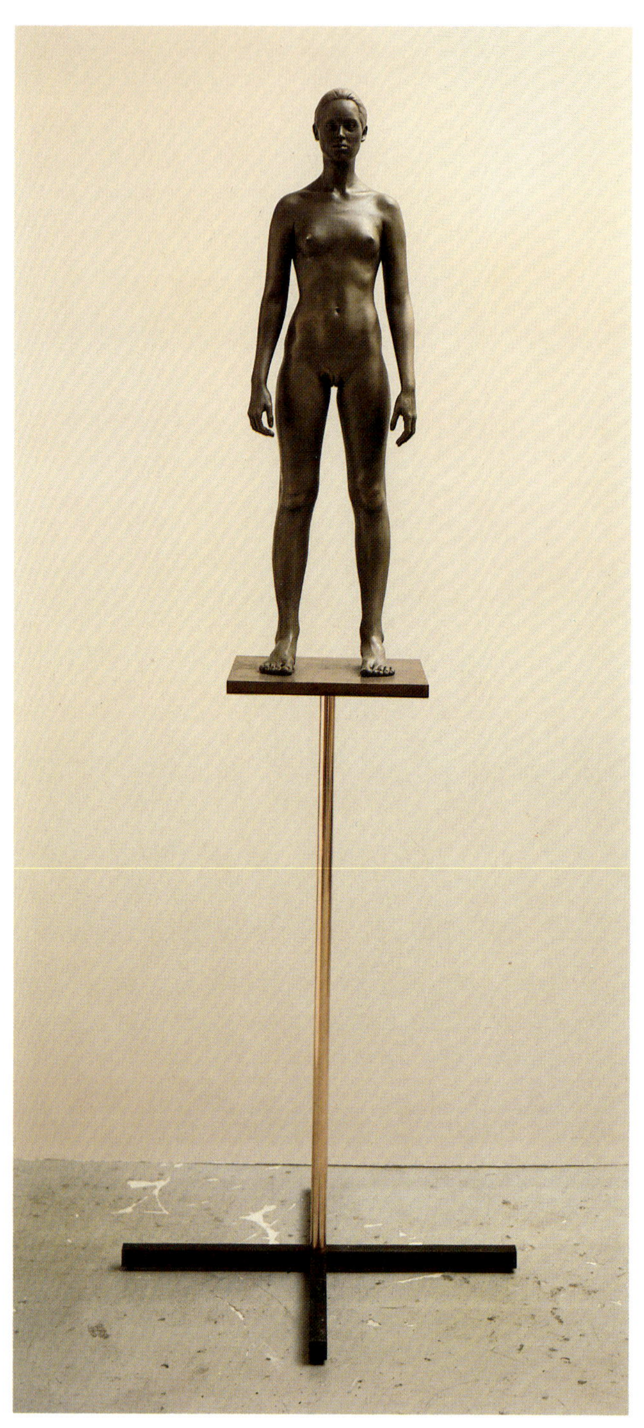

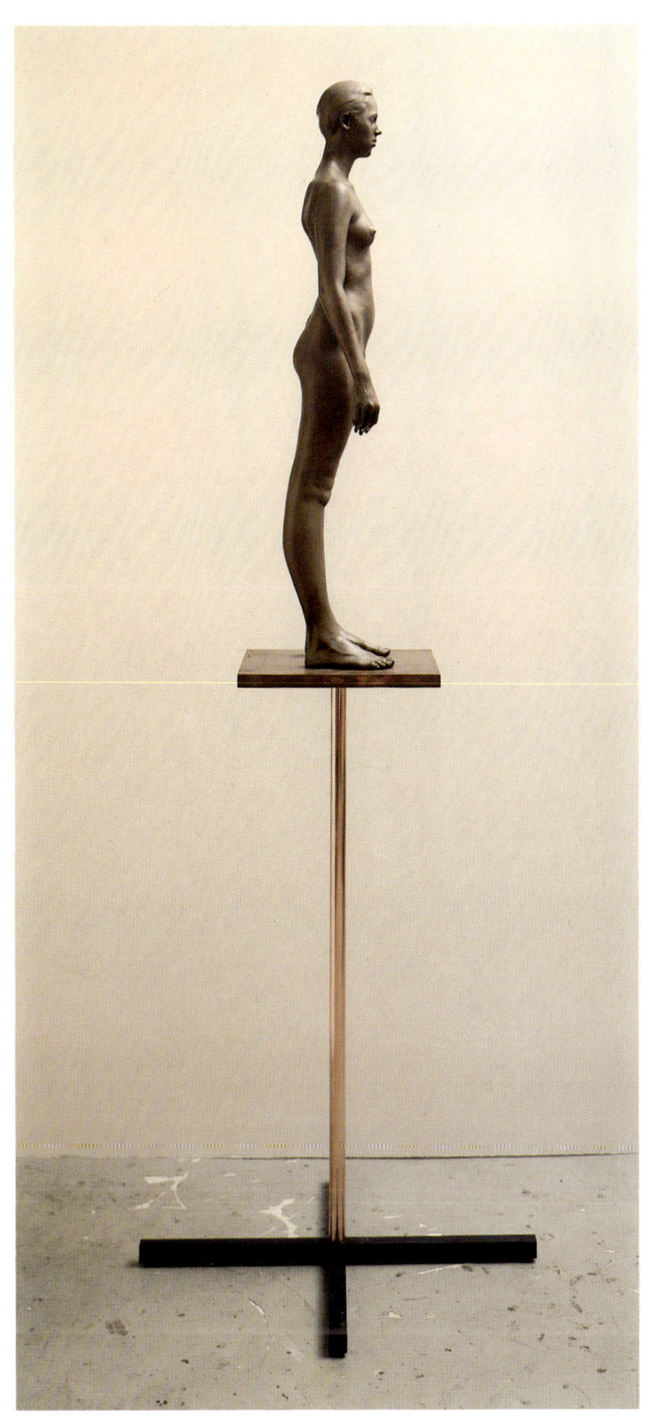

Cherie   1980
bronze
71¼ x 10½ x 6¼
Courtesy Dorothy Rosenthal Gallery

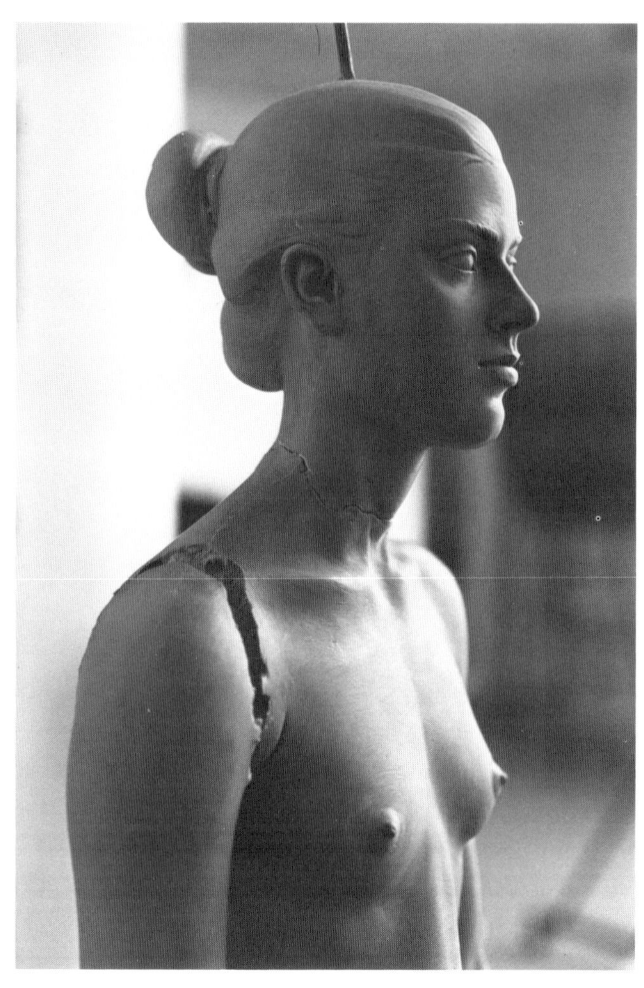

WORKING METHOD

George W. Neubert

While there is general understanding of most traditional procedures and techniques involved in sculpture, such as modeling and firing of clay and the carving of stone, the transformation from an artist's clay model to its permanent bronze replica has always been somewhat mysterious.

The process utilized by Robert Graham is known as the *cire perdue* (lost wax) casting method. The basic techniques and methods employed in this procedure were developed centuries ago. Now, using advanced techniques and new materials and methods, Graham has adopted this complex historical process to achieve his highly-crafted bronze statues. The first stage of the process is the modeling of the figure in wet clay; this is done in relief, one-half of the figure at a time (usually the front half first), on a flat surface. Once this first half is completed, Graham forms a plaster "mother" mold over that half figure. Turning over the plaster mold he then uses the clay as an outline to

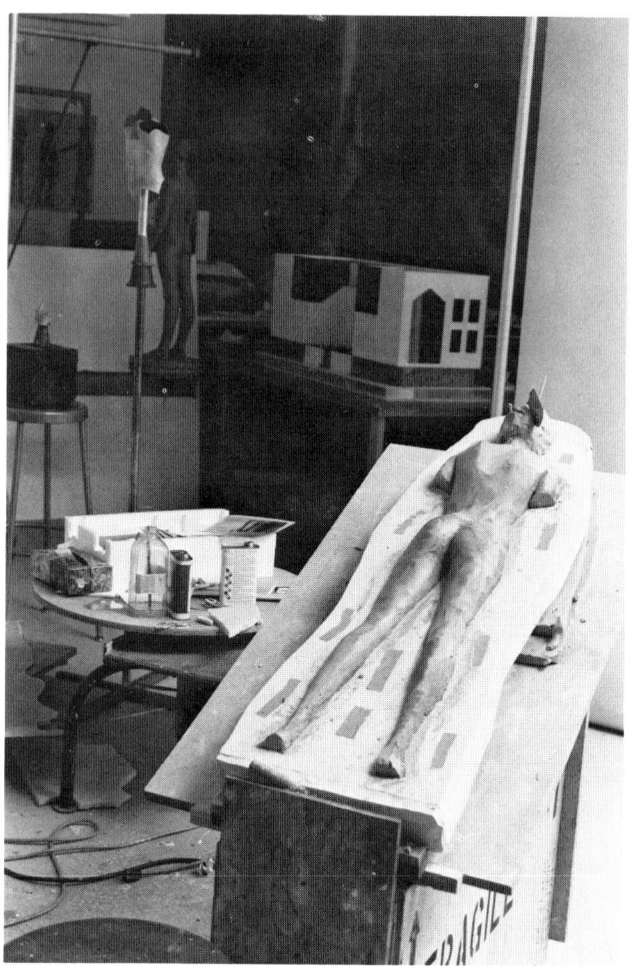

complete the second half of the full figure. This procedure provides for Graham a certain directness and speed that conventional methods do not allow. This half-relief technique eliminates the necessity of an armature in the wet clay and the normal fighting of gravity.

Once the second half of the figure is complete, Graham forms a matching plaster cast creating a two-part mold or shell. It is then separated and the clay is removed, destroying the original figure in the process. This "mother" mold creates a negative impression of the artist's original clay model. Within the hollow mold a wire armature is formed, conforming to the figure shape but not touching the mold surface. The mold is then closed again and plasticine poured into it forming a master figure. This is the second stage of the modeling process.

Graham now has a master figure of plasticine with a wire armature that is suspended from its head.

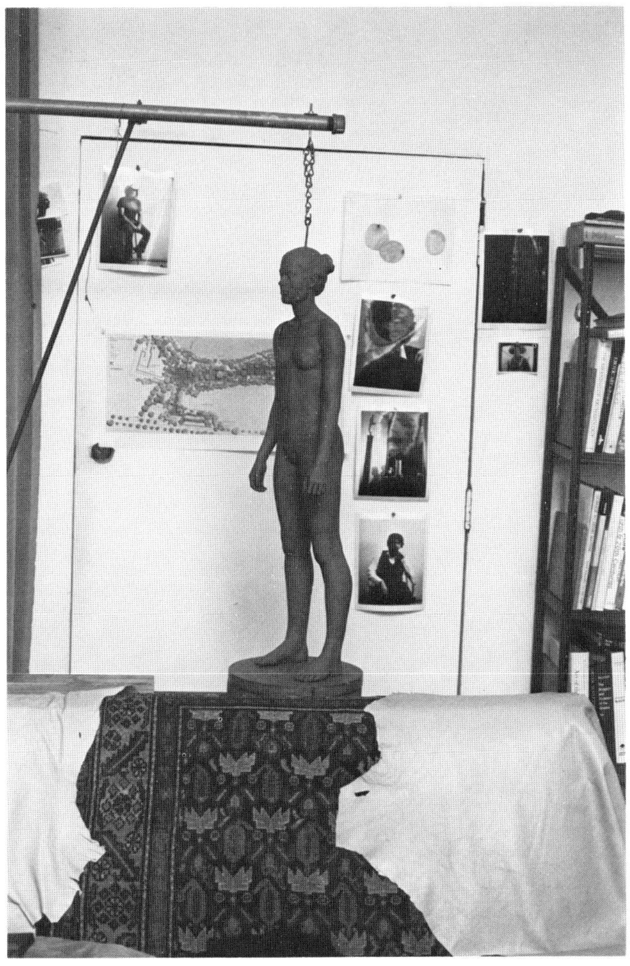

Working from a live model again Graham further refines the hanging figure until he achieves the desired posture and feeling of the model. Once the final configuration is determined, another mold is made of this newly finished figure. This master mold is made of latex rubber and is used as the basis for the series of wax patterns essential to the bronze casting process. For this, molten wax is poured into the rubber mold, sloshed around the hollow interior and permitted to coagulate, forming a hollow wax shell figure on the surface of the mold. Excess wax is poured out.

At this stage Graham has a perfect replica—or pattern—of the sculpture in wax. This wax pattern is usually cut in half; wax rods—sprues—and air vents are then attached to the wax fragments. The sprues all lead from the figure to a cone-shaped entrance that forms the opening to all parts of the pattern. This configuration is repeatedly dipped with great care into a ceramic liquid that sets and forms an "investment shell" around the wax pattern—inside and out. This ceramic investment is then fired in a kiln hardening the shell. The wax is melted by the heat—"lost"—leaving a hollow pattern of the original wax model. Next, molten bronze (at just under 2000 degrees fahrenheit) is poured into the investment shell, filling the hollow core—in other words, whatever was wax, is now filled with bronze. Within minutes, the bronze sets and hardens and the ceramic shell (referred to as the waste mold) can then be broken away.

For the next stage in the process, control and craftsmanship is as important as it was in the original modeling. This is the "phasing" or refinishing and re-surfacing of the bronze sculpture that Graham insists on doing himself to assure no loss of surface definition. First, all of the sprues and air vents must be cut away. The figure fragments are then welded back together to re-form the figure in bronze. The welded seams are filed, the imperfections are smoothed and the surface is cleaned and polished. Sometimes, as in the Fragments, Graham does not remove all the circulatory systems (air vents and pouring cone), but retains them as part of the finished work.

The final stage is the determination of the bronze surface coloration. Traditionally, color has been applied with a patina—that is, chemically con-trolled oxidation of the bronze surface, as seen in Gra-ham's earlier bronze work. In recent work, he has often negated the original surface by painting over the bronze with pale tones of oil paint. He has indicated that his interest is not in color, but in surface and says, "It has to do with reflecting the light back and with a consistency of image and the statue's surface."

To provide total control of this complicated and technical procedure, Robert Graham has set up a complete foundry facility in his California studio. The artisanship and technical standards achieved by Ro-bert Graham in his *cire perdue* bronze statues proves once again that individual achievement can reassert the validity of a long-neglected form.

George W. Neubert is Associate Director of Art, San Francisco Museum of Modern Art.

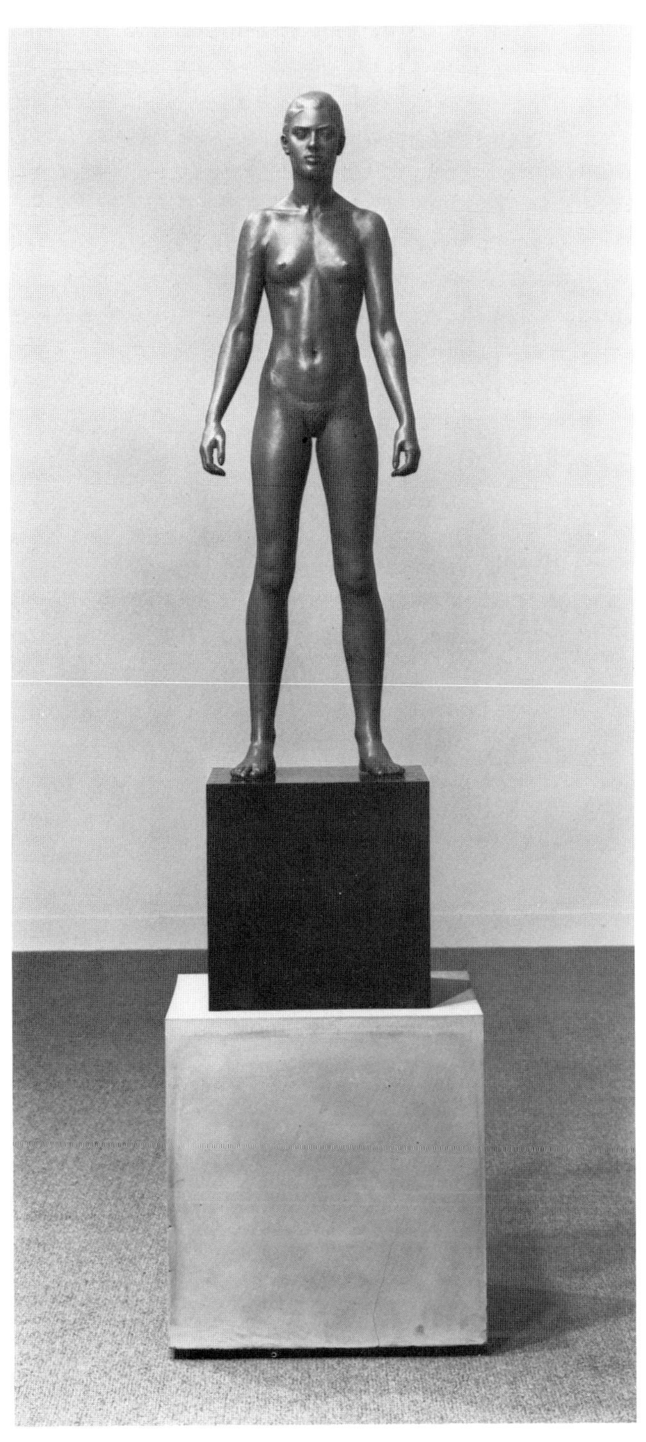

Stephanie   1980
bronze
69½ x 11½ x 7½
Courtesy Robert Miller Gallery

Biography

1938
Born in Mexico City.

1961-63
Studied at San Jose State College.

1963-64
Attended San Francisco Art Institute.

1964-69
Lived and worked in Los Angeles.

1966
Created diminutive wax figures, placed in plexiglass box environments.

1969-70
Lived and worked mainly in London.

1971
Returned to Los Angeles and began casting his sculptures in bronze.

1978
Selected as one of four artists to work on the proposed FDR Memorial, Washington, D.C.

1981
Lives and works in Venice, California.

One-Artist Exhibitions

1964
Lanyon Gallery, Palo Alto

1966
Nicholas Wilder Gallery, Los Angeles

1967
Galerie Thelen, Essen, West Germany

1968
Kornblee Gallery, New York
Galerie Neuendorf, Hamburg and Cologne
Galerie Zwirner, Cologne

1969
Kornblee Gallery, New York

1970
Galerie Neuendorf, Hamburg and Cologne
Galerie Mollenhoff, Cologne
Galerie Rene Black, Berlin
Whitechapel Gallery, London

1971
Sonnabend Gallery, New York
Kunstverein, Hamburg

1972
Galerie Herbert Meyer-Ellinger, Frankfurt
Dallas Museum of Fine Arts

1974
Nicholas Wilder Gallery, Los Angeles
Galerie Neuendorf, Hamburg and Cologne
Galerie Zwirner, Cologne
Felicity Samuel Gallery, London
Gimpel & Hannover Gallery, Zurich

1975
Nicholas Wilder Gallery, Los Angeles
Gimpel & Hannover Gallery, Zurich
Gimpel & Hannover Gallery, Basel Art Fair
Dorothy Rosenthal Gallery, Chicago
Texas Gallery, Houston
Greenberg Gallery, St. Louis

1976
Galerie Neuendorf, Hamburg
Gimpel Fils, London

1977
Robert Miller Gallery, New York
Nicholas Wilder Gallery, Los Angeles
John Stoller Gallery, Minneapolis

1979, 1980
Robert Miller Gallery, New York

1981
Los Angeles County Museum of Art

Selected Group Exhibitions

1966, 1969, 1971, 1979
Exhibitions at the Whitney Museum of American Art,
New York

1969
Washington University Gallery of Art, St. Louis,
Here and Now

1971
Victoria and Albert Museum, London, *Three Americans*

1972
Kunstverein in Hamburg, Hannover, Cologne,
Stuttgart, *West Coast USA*

1975
Smithsonian Institution, Washington, D.C.,
Sculpture—American Directions 1945-1975

1976
Los Angeles County Museum of Art,
Los Angeles—Eight Artists
San Francisco Museum of Modern Art,
Painting and Sculpture in California

1978
Rutgers University Art Gallery, New Brunswick, New Jersey,
Contemporary Artist Series Number 1

Selected Bibliography

Articles and Reviews

1966
Aldrich, Larry. "New Talent USA," *Art in America*, July-August 1966, p 65.

Factor, Don. "Los Angeles: Robert Graham, Nicholas Wilder Gallery," *Artforum*, April 1966, p 14.

Metcalf, Katherine. "Art News from San Francisco," *Art News*, Summer 1966, p 55.

1967
Danieli, Fidel A. "Los Angeles: Robert Graham, Nicholas Wilder Gallery," *Artforum*, April 1967, p 62.

1968
Pincus-Witten, Robert. "New York: Robert Graham, Kornblee Gallery," *Artforum*, Summer 1968, p 52.

1969
Nemser, Cindy. "In the Galleries: Robert Graham at Kornblee Gallery," *Arts Magazine*, May 1969, p 64.

1970
Russell, David. "London," *Arts Magazine*, September-October 1970, p 56.

Winer, Helene. "Robert Graham's Boxes," *Studio International* May 1970, pp 216-217.

1971
Elderfield, John. "New York: Robert Graham, Sonnabend Gallery," *Artforum*, March 1971, pp 67-68.

Henry, Gerrit. "Reviews and Previews: Robert Graham at Sonnabend," *Art News*, March 1971, p 20.

Marandel, J. Patrice. "Lettre de New York," *Art International*, 20 March 1971, pp 55-56.

Masheck, Joseph. "Sorting out the Whitney Annual," *Artforum*, February 1971, p 74.

1972
Dienst, R.G. "Robert Graham," *Das Kunstwerk*, January 1972, pp 20-28.

1974
Wilson, W. "California Report," *Domus*, November 1974, p 49.

1976
Morrison, C.L. "Robert Graham at Dorothy Rosenthal Gallery, Chicago," *Artforum*, February 1976, p 67.

Ratcliff, Carter. "Notes on Small Sculpture," *Artforum*, April 1976, pp 39-40.

1977
Ellenzweig, Allan. "Robert Graham at Robert Miller," *Arts Magazine*, December 1977, pp 19-20.

Kramer, Hilton. "Art: Modernists Brake for Tradition," *New York Times*, 14 October 1977.

1978
Carter, Malcolm. "The FDR Memorial," *Art News*, October 1978, pp 50-57.

Rubenfein, Leo. "West Coast Artists," *Art in America*, September 1978, p 81.

1979
Glueck, Grace. "The Renaissance Sculptor for Roosevelt Memorial," *New York Times*, 6 May 1979.

Isenberg, Barbara. "Robert Graham: Ignoring the Lessons of Modern Art," *Art News*, January 1979, pp 66-69.

Kramer, Hilton. *New York Times*, 9 November 1979.

Zimmer, William. "Who Puts Women on a Pedestal?" *Soho Weekly News*, 15 November 1979.

1980
Friedman, Jon. "Robert Graham at Robert Miller Gallery," *Arts Magazine*, January 1980, p 38.

Lawson, T. "Robert Miller Gallery, New York," *Flash Art*, January-February 1980, p 26.

Books and Catalogues

1968
Finch, Christopher. *Pop Art: Object and Image.* E.P. Dutton and Co., Inc., New York, pp 60-64.

Kultermann, Udo. *The New Sculpture: Environments and Assemblages.* Frederick A. Praeger, New York, pp 30-35.

1970
Robert Graham: Works 1963-1969. Buchhandlung Walther Konig, Cologne.

Glazebrook, Mark.*Robert Graham.* The Whitechapel Art Gallery, London.

1972
Murdock, Robert. *Robert Graham.* Dallas Museum of Fine Arts.

USA West Coast. Kunstverein in Hamburg, pp 53-57.

1976
Los Angeles-Eight Artists: Painting and Sculpture 1976. Los Angeles County Museum of Art.

1977
Painting and Sculpture in California: The Modern Era. San Francisco Museum of Modern Art.

1978
Wechsler, Jeffrey. *Robert Graham: Contemporary Artist Series Number 1*, Rutgers University Art Gallery, New Jersey, pp 1-4.

Walker Art Center
Staff for the Exhibition

Registrar
Gwen Bitz
Graphic Design
Robert Jensen
Michael Cervantes,
Walker Art Center/Ellerbe Design Intern
Don Bergh
Catalogue
Mildred S. Friedman
Linda Krenzin
Mary Mancuso
Installation
Hugh Jacobson
Tom Briggs
Steve Ecklund
Ron Elliott
Mary Gstalder
Joe Janson
John King
Cody Riddle
Public Information
Mary Abbe Martin
Karen Statler
Research Assistance
Sarah Rogers, Abby Grey Fellow,
National Endowment for the Arts Intern

Photo Credits

Malcolm Lubliner: pp 6, 10, 13, 15, 18-21,
23-27, 29, 32-37, 43
Eric Sutherland: p 8
Frank Thomas: p 11
Graham Beal: pp 30, 38, 40, 41

Colophon

This catalogue was printed on Quintessence papers
by Colormaster Press.
The type is Sabon
and was set at Walker Art Center
on a Mergenthaler CRTronic.
The binding is by Midwest Editions.
The design is by Robert Jensen.